WHEN ANIMALS ATTACK

Contents

Watch Out! Animals About! 2

Anaconda 4

Great White Shark 6

Grizzly Bear 10

Hippopotamus 12

Leopard 14

Mountain Gorilla 16

Saltwater Crocodile 20

Tiger 22

Glossary 24

Written by Paul Mason

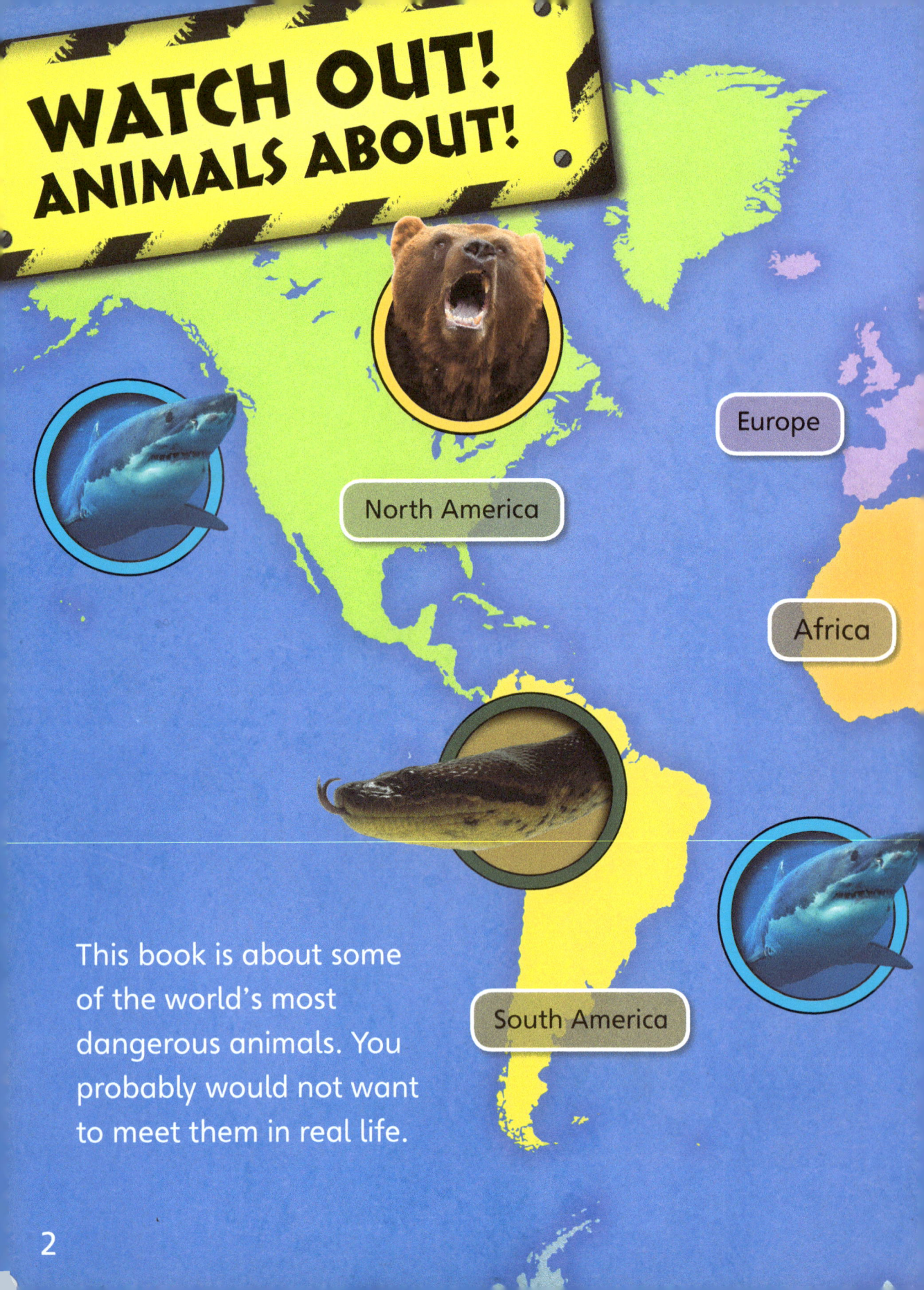

WATCH OUT! ANIMALS ABOUT!

Europe

North America

Africa

South America

This book is about some of the world's most dangerous animals. You probably would not want to meet them in real life.

Asia

Australia

What if you *were* attacked by any of these animals, though? This guide tells you how to give yourself the best chance of staying alive!

3

ANACONDA

The green anaconda is the world's biggest snake. It can easily squeeze the breath from a person!

The anaconda attacks from shallow water, such as rivers and deep puddles.

If An Anaconda Attacks

Fight back! Bite the tip of the snake's tail hard, or beat its head with a rock. It may decide to look for an easier meal.

FACT FILE

Weight: 225 kg

Length: up to 9 m

GREAT WHITE SHARK

Nose can smell blood from 5 **kilometres** (km) away

Sensors along the shark's sides feel **electric signals** from its prey

300 razor-sharp teeth

This is one fish you do *not* want to meet! About half of all shark attacks are probably by great whites.

If you see a great white's fin **circling** you in the water, what should you do?

FACT FILE

Weight: 2 tonnes

Length: up to 6 m

Top speed: 25 km an hour

Avoid Becoming A Shark Snack

1. Make sure you know where the shark is. Sharks often attack from below or behind.

2. Shout for help from nearby boats.

> Yum, lunch! A great white's favourite food isn't a swimmer – it's a seal.

3. If the shark comes close, hit its eyes, **gills**, and nose.

4. If the shark disappears, look down into the water with the sun behind you. That is where the attack will come from.

5. If a shark attacks, wriggle and twist to avoid it.

The diver is glad he is safe inside the cage!

GRIZZLY BEAR

If a grizzly charges at you, your only hope is to curl into a ball and **play dead**!

Powerful bite

Arms can tear off a car door

Claws can rip through metal

FACT FILE

Weight: 350 kg

Length: up to 2.5 m

Top speed: 48 km an hour

If You Meet A Grizzly

If the bear is a long way away, start talking loudly. Some people even sing! The bear usually goes away.

If you meet a grizzly up close, move backwards slowly. Do not turn around, but do not look straight at the bear.

This bear is looking for some food.

HIPPOPOTAMUS

The hippopotamus is Africa's deadliest animal. It kills more people than lions, leopards or crocodiles.

Teeth up to 50 cm long

Really strong jaws

Top Tips For Avoiding A Hippo Attack

1. Never get between a hippo and the water.

2. If chased, hide behind a tree.

3. Never get between a mother hippo and her baby – she *will* attack you.

FACT FILE

Weight: 3500 kg

Length: up to 5 m

Top speed: 40 km an hour

LEOPARD

Leopards are hard to spot: you can be almost on top of one without realizing it.

FACT FILE

Weight: 80 kg

Length: up to 3.3 m with tail

Top speed: 60 km an hour

Leopards hunt using surprise attacks. Their **camouflage** makes them hard to see.

Avoid Becoming Leopard Lunch!

If you meet a leopard:

- do not run away – it will chase you

- stare at it – in the cat world this is a sign of **aggression**

- make yourself look big

- shout loudly but calmly.

All this may make the leopard decide to look for easier prey.

Leopards start learning to hunt when they are very young.

MOUNTAIN GORILLA

Mountain gorillas live in small groups. The silverback is the leader.

The silverback keeps a lookout for strangers.

The silverback's jobs include:

- finding the best leaves to eat
- picking a place to nest at night
- defending the group's **territory**.

If you wander into his territory, the silverback might attack!

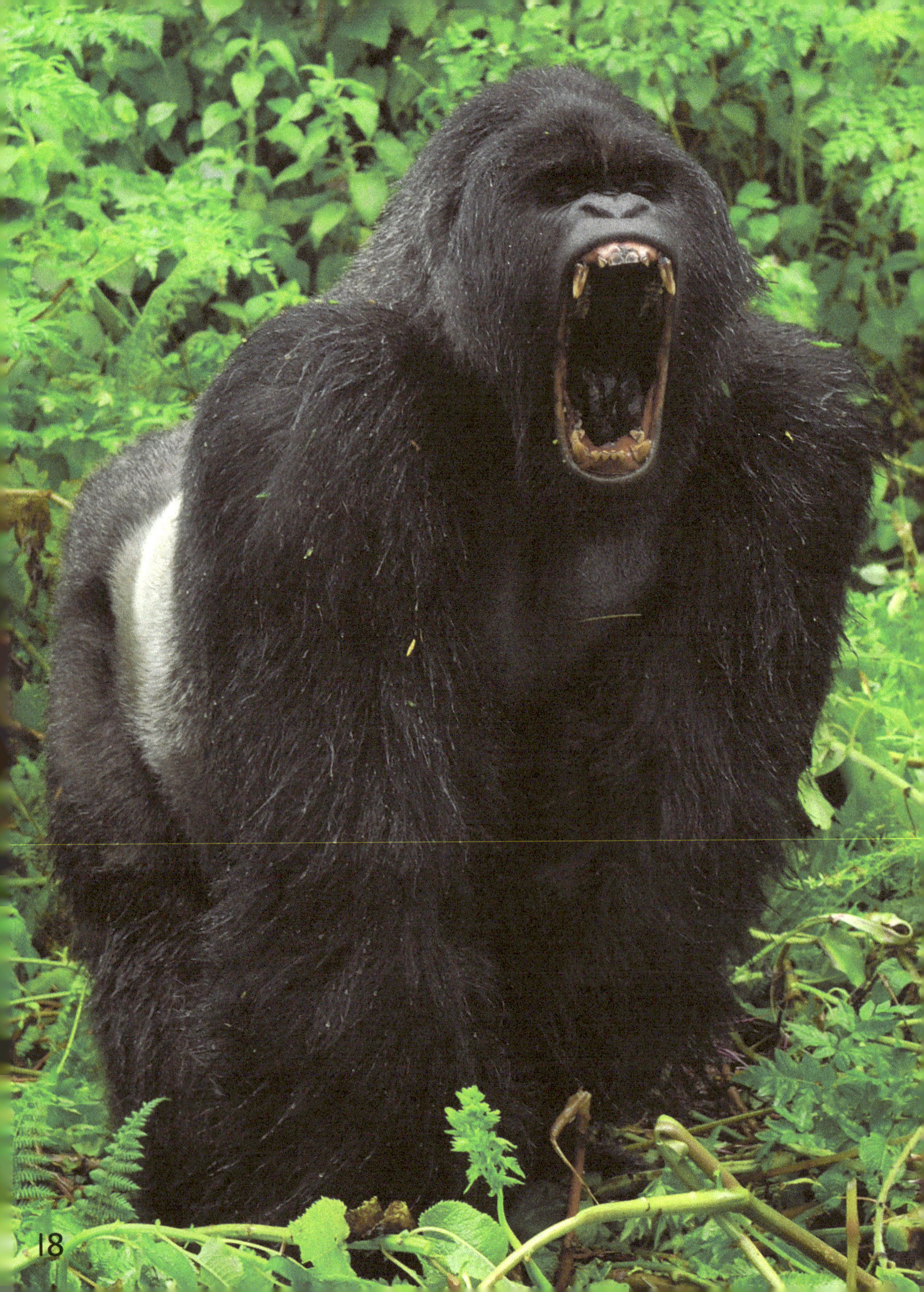

If You Annoy a Gorilla

When he is about to attack, a silverback hoots, throws plants, stands up, and beats his chest. What should you do?

1. Look down at the ground, to one side.

2. Walk backwards slowly, until you can no longer see him.

3. Once out of sight, get away as quickly as possible!

FACT FILE

Weight: 200 kg

Length: up to 1.9 m

Top speed: 30 km an hour – faster than you!

SALTWATER CROCODILE

To a saltwater crocodile, a water buffalo or a monkey is a tasty snack. It grabs its **victim** and pulls it underwater.

A saltwater crocodile can easily **crush** a human's skull in one bite.

Do Not Be a Salty's Snack!

1. Stay away from the water's edge.
2. Never turn your back on the water. Salties like to attack when their prey isn't looking!
3. If chased, run away fast. Crocodiles are very good swimmers but are slower on land!

FACT FILE

Weight: 450 kg

Length: 5 m

Top speed:
17 km an hour on land, 40 km an hour when attacking from water

TIGER

A hungry tiger eats 27 kg of meat a night. That's 240 burgers!

Strong back legs can leap 10 metres

Long claws (10–12 cm) for gripping prey

Anti-tiger action

Tigers creep up behind their prey. If a tiger is around, wear a mask on the back of your head. This will fool the tiger into thinking you can see it. It will not attack!

Powerful jaws for biting prey's neck

FACT FILE

Weight: 300 kg

Length: 3.3 m

Top speed: 55 km an hour

GLOSSARY

aggression — wish to fight or attack

camouflage — colours or markings on an animal's coat that help it to blend into the background

circling — moving around something, staying the same distance from it all the time

crush — squash down into a flattened shape

electric signals — tiny flashes of electricity that animals' nerves give off whenever they move

gills — what fish use to breathe

kilometres — 1 kilometre is 1000 metres

play dead — lie still, curled into a ball, pretending to be dead

territory — home area, where an animal lives and hunts

victim — living creatures that are hurt or killed